The Ultimate Guide to Self Reiki Healing: A Step-by-Step Handbook for Beginners Bonus Chapter Reiki for Pets

Copyright © 2023 by Posh My Gosh, Inc.
All rights reserved

Title: The Ultimate Guide to Self Reiki Healing: A Step-by-Step Handbook for Beginners Bonus Chapter Reiki for Pets

This publication is intended for informational purposes only. The information contained in this book is not intended to diagnose, treat, cure, or prevent any disease or medical condition. The content is intended to provide general information about Reiki and self-healing practices.

No part of this book may be reproduced in any form by any electronic or mechanical means, including information storage or retrieval systems, without permission in writing from the publisher. The material in this book is protected by copyright laws and intellectual property rights.

The information in this book is based on the author's personal experiences and research and should not be taken as a substitute for professional medical advice or treatment. It is recommended that you consult with a qualified healthcare practitioner before beginning any new self-healing practices.

The author and publisher of this book are not responsible for any adverse effects or consequences resulting from the use of the information provided in this book. The reader assumes full responsibility for their use of the information in this book.

While every effort has been made to ensure the accuracy and completeness of the information contained in this book, the author and publisher make no representations or warranties of any kind, express or implied, about the completeness, accuracy, reliability, suitability, or availability with respect to the information, products, services, or related graphics contained in this book for any purpose. Any reliance you place on such information is therefore strictly at your own risk.

In conclusion, this book is a guide to self-healing practices using Reiki. It is important to understand that the information contained in this book is intended for informational purposes only and should not be used as a substitute for professional medical advice. The author and publisher are not responsible for any adverse effects or consequences resulting from the use of this information. Please consult with a qualified healthcare practitioner before beginning any new self-healing practices.

ISBN: 9798396050815

Imprint: Independently published

For information on and a full description of other Kulada Zaire products please visit www.kulada.com

CONTENTS

Chapter 1: Understanding Reiki Healing
- What is Reiki?
- The History of Reiki
- How Does Reiki Work?
- The Benefits of Reiki

Chapter 2: Preparing for Self Reiki Healing
- Creating a Sacred Space
- Setting Your Intention
- Grounding Yourself
- Clearing Your Energy

Chapter 3: Learning the Reiki Hand Positions
- Hand Positions for Self Reiki
- Hand Positions for Treating Others
- The Importance of Intuition in Reiki

Chapter 4: Starting Your Self Reiki Practice
- Step-by-Step Guide to Self Reiki
- Tips for Enhancing Your Self Reiki Practice
- Recommended Self Reiki Practices

Chapter 5: Troubleshooting Your Self Reiki Practice
- Common Challenges in Self Reiki

- How to Overcome Blockages in Your Energy Flow
- The Role of Reiki Practitioners in Supporting Your Practice

Chapter 6: Incorporating Reiki into Your Daily Life
- Using Reiki for Stress Management
- Reiki for Improved Sleep
- Reiki for Enhanced Creativity and Productivity

Chapter 7: Reiki For Pets
- The Benefits of Reiki for Animals
- How to Give Reiki to Your Pets
- Case Studies: Reiki for Pets with Health Issues

INTRODUCTION

Introducing "The Ultimate Guide to Self Reiki Healing: A Step-by-Step Handbook for Beginners + Bonus Chapter Reiki for Pets"

Are you looking for a natural and holistic way to improve your physical, emotional, and spiritual well-being? If so, then Reiki may be the answer you've been searching for. Reiki is a Japanese healing modality that uses universal life force energy to balance and harmonize the body, mind, and spirit.

"The Ultimate Guide to Self Reiki Healing: A Step-by-Step Handbook for Beginners + Bonus Chapter Reiki for Pets" is the perfect resource for anyone who wants to learn the art of Reiki. This comprehensive guide is designed to provide you with everything you need to know about Reiki, from its history and benefits to step-by-step instructions for practicing Reiki on yourself and others.

In this book, you will learn how to:

- Prepare for self Reiki healing by creating a sacred space, setting your intention, grounding yourself, and clearing your energy
- Practice Reiki on yourself using the hand positions and recommended self Reiki practices
- Troubleshoot common challenges in self Reiki and overcome blockages in your energy flow
- Incorporate Reiki into your daily life to manage stress, improve sleep, and enhance creativity and productivity
- Give Reiki to your pets and experience the benefits of Reiki for animals

With the bonus chapter on Reiki for pets, you will also learn how to give Reiki to your furry friends and help them heal from health issues.

"The Ultimate Guide to Self Reiki Healing: A Step-by-Step Handbook for Beginners + Bonus Chapter Reiki for Pets" is written in a clear and concise manner, making it easy for anyone to understand and practice Reiki. Whether you are new to Reiki or a seasoned practitioner, this book is a valuable resource to add to your healing toolkit.

So, if you're ready to experience the transformative power of Reiki, then read "The Ultimate Guide to

Self Reiki Healing: A Step-by-Step Handbook for Beginners + Bonus Chapter Reiki for Pets" today!

Reiki is a natural healing technique that promotes relaxation, stress reduction, and overall well-being. It is a Japanese method of healing that involves the transfer of energy from the practitioner's hands to the patient's body. One of the best things about Reiki is that anyone can learn it, and it can be practiced anywhere, at any time. In this e-book, we will guide you through the process of self Reiki healing, a practice that involves using Reiki on yourself to promote healing and well-being.

Once upon a time, there was a woman named Sarah who had been feeling stressed and overwhelmed for weeks. Her job was demanding, her family was going through a difficult time, and she felt like she was constantly running on empty. One day, Sarah decided to try self Reiki healing as a way to calm her mind and find some peace.

She found a quiet, comfortable spot in her home and began to practice self Reiki. She placed her hands on her head, feeling the warmth and energy flow through her. She moved her hands down to her neck and shoulders, feeling the tension melt away. As she continued to move her hands down her body, she felt a sense of deep relaxation and calm wash over her.

As she held her hands on her heart center, she began to feel a sense of love and compassion for herself. She realized that she had been pushing herself too hard and neglecting her own needs. With each position, she felt more and more connected to herself and to the present moment.

When she finished the self Reiki session, she felt renewed and refreshed. Her mind was clear and her body felt lighter. She felt more confident in her ability to handle the challenges of her life and more connected to her own inner wisdom.

From that day on, Sarah made self Reiki a regular part of her self-care routine. Whenever she felt stressed or overwhelmed, she would find a quiet spot and practice self Reiki. It became a powerful tool for her to connect with herself, find peace, and promote her own well-being.

In the end, Sarah discovered that the practice of self Reiki healing was not just a way to heal her body and mind, but a way to connect with her inner self and cultivate a deeper sense of peace and harmony in her life.

Chapter 1: Understanding Reiki Healing

In this chapter, we will introduce you to the concept of Reiki, its history, and how it works. We will also discuss the benefits of Reiki healing and why it is important to practice it regularly.

1. Reiki healing is a Japanese technique for stress reduction and relaxation that also promotes healing. Reiki healing is an ancient Japanese technique that has been used for centuries to promote healing, relaxation, and stress reduction. The word
Reiki comes from two Japanese words - "rei," which means universal, and "ki," which means life force energy. Reiki is a form of energy healing that works by channeling this life force energy through the hands of the practitioner and into the body of the recipient.

Reiki healing is a non-invasive therapy that is performed with the recipient fully clothed and lying down or seated. The practitioner begins by placing their hands on or near the recipient's body in a series of hand positions, starting at the head and moving down to the feet. The practitioner then channels the energy into the recipient's body, promoting the flow of energy and removing any blockages that may be causing physical or emotional discomfort.

Reiki healing is a gentle and soothing process that can be used to treat a wide range of physical and emotional conditions. It is often used to help reduce stress, anxiety, and depression, and can be helpful in managing chronic pain, promoting relaxation, and improving overall health and well-being.

Reiki healing is based on the belief that illness and disease are caused by imbalances in the body's energy system. By restoring balance to the body's energy, Reiki healing can help to promote healing and relieve symptoms of illness and disease.

Overall, Reiki healing is a powerful and effective way to promote healing, relaxation, and stress reduction. Whether you are looking to improve your physical health, manage chronic pain, or simply find a way to relax and unwind, Reiki healing can be a valuable tool in your journey towards health and wellness.

2. Reiki is based on the idea that an unseen life force energy flows through us and is what causes us to be alive.

Reiki is a healing technique that is based on the idea that there is a life force energy that flows through all living things. This energy is known as "ki" in Japan, "chi" in China, and "prana" in India. The belief in this life force energy is rooted in many ancient cultures and is a central concept in many traditional healing practices.

The idea behind Reiki healing is that this life force energy can become blocked or disrupted, leading to physical or emotional imbalances. When this happens, the body's natural ability to heal itself is compromised. Reiki practitioners believe that by channeling this energy into the body, they can help to remove these blockages and restore balance to the body's energy system.

Reiki practitioners believe that this life force energy is not visible to the naked eye, but can be felt and sensed through the hands. They believe that by placing their hands on or near a person's body, they can channel this energy into the person, promoting healing and restoring balance.

There is no scientific evidence to support the existence of this life force energy, and some skeptics have dismissed Reiki as a pseudoscientific practice. However, many people who have received Reiki treatments report feeling more relaxed, less stressed, and more at peace. Some people also report feeling physical sensations such as warmth or tingling during a Reiki session.

Regardless of whether or not the existence of this life force energy can be scientifically proven, many people find Reiki to be a helpful tool in promoting relaxation and healing. Reiki can be used in conjunction with other forms of medical treatment, and is often used as a complementary therapy to help manage symptoms of chronic illness or stress.

3. Reiki is a healing practice founded by Mikao Usui in the early 1900s in Japan. Usui was a spiritual teacher who developed the practice after spending many years studying various healing techniques and spiritual

practices. He believed that by channeling energy through the hands of a practitioner, it could promote physical, emotional, and spiritual healing in the body.

The word Reiki is derived from the Japanese words "rei" (meaning universal) and "ki" (meaning life energy). In Reiki, practitioners use their hands to channel this life energy to promote healing in the body. The practice is based on the belief that we all have a life force energy that flows through us, and that when this energy is blocked or disrupted, it can lead to physical and emotional imbalances. During a Reiki session, the practitioner will place their hands on or near the client's body, using a series of hand positions. The practitioner will then channel energy through their hands, directing it to the areas of the body that need healing. The client may feel a warm or tingling sensation during the session, and many people report feeling relaxed and peaceful.

Reiki is often used to treat a variety of physical and emotional conditions, including stress, anxiety, chronic pain, and insomnia. It is also used to promote overall wellness and balance in the body. Reiki is often used as a complementary therapy to traditional medical treatments, and many hospitals and clinics now offer Reiki as a part of their healing services.

Today, Reiki has become a popular healing practice around the world, and there are many different styles and techniques used by practitioners. While the practice has evolved since its founding, the basic principles of channeling energy through the hands to promote healing remain at the core of the Reiki philosophy.

4. The principles of Reiki are based on the idea that promoting harmony and balance in the body can help to promote healing. The principles of Reiki are often referred to as the Five Reiki Principles or the Five Reiki Precepts, and they are an essential part of the Reiki practice.

The Five Reiki Principles are:

1. Just for today, I will not be angry.

2. Just for today, I will not worry.

3. Just for today, I will be grateful.

4. Just for today, I will do my work honestly.

5. Just for today, I will be kind to every living thing.

These principles are meant to be a guide for living a more balanced and harmonious life. By focusing on these principles, Reiki practitioners aim to promote a sense of peace and well-being in their daily lives.
The first principle, "just for today, I will not be angry," encourages practitioners to let go of negative emotions and to avoid getting caught up in anger or frustration. By releasing negative emotions, practitioners can create a more peaceful and calm state of mind.

The second principle, "just for today, I will not worry," encourages practitioners to focus on the present moment and to let go of worries and anxieties about the future. By focusing on the present, practitioners can reduce stress and anxiety and create a more peaceful state of mind.

The third principle, "just for today, I will be

grateful," encourages practitioners to cultivate a sense of gratitude for all the blessings in their lives. By focusing on gratitude, practitioners can create a more positive mindset and attract more positivity into their lives.

The fourth principle, "just for today, I will do my work honestly," encourages practitioners to be honest and transparent in all their dealings. By being honest, practitioners can create more trust and respect in their relationships and create a more positive environment around them.

The fifth principle, "just for today, I will be kind to every living thing," encourages practitioners to cultivate a sense of kindness and compassion towards all living beings.

5. Following the principles of Reiki can have a profound impact on our mental and emotional well-being. When we focus on the present moment, let go of negative emotions and thoughts, and cultivate a sense of gratitude and kindness, we can create a more positive and peaceful environment within ourselves and around us.

By focusing on the present moment, we can let go of worries and anxieties about the future or regrets about the past. This can help reduce stress and anxiety and promote a sense of calm and well-being. When we let go of negative emotions and thoughts, we create space for more positive and uplifting energies to flow through us, which can help us feel more positive and optimistic.

Cultivating a sense of gratitude and kindness can also have a profound impact on our mental and emotional well-being. When we focus on the blessings in our lives and cultivate a sense of gratitude, we can create a more positive and abundant mindset. This can help us feel more content and fulfilled, even during challenging times.

Similarly, when we cultivate a sense of kindness and compassion towards all living beings, we promote a sense of harmony and balance in the world around us. This can help us feel more connected to others and to the world at large, which can promote a sense of inner peace and well-being.

Overall, following the principles of Reiki can help us create a more positive and peaceful environment within ourselves and around us. By focusing on the present moment, letting go of negative emotions and thoughts, and cultivating a sense of gratitude and kindness, we can promote an overall sense of calm, well-being, and harmony in our lives.

6. Reiki healing is a non-invasive, holistic approach to healing that aims to promote balance and harmony within the body and mind. The practice of Reiki involves the use of hands-on or distance healing techniques to channel energy into the body, promoting relaxation and reducing stress and anxiety. The benefits of Reiki healing are numerous and can have a profound impact on our physical, emotional, and mental well-being.

One of the most significant benefits of Reiki healing is its ability to reduce stress and anxiety. The practice of Reiki promotes deep relaxation, which can help reduce feelings of stress and anxiety. By promoting relaxation, Reiki also helps to lower blood pressure, reduce heart rate, and calm the nervous system. This can help to improve our overall sense of well-being and promote a more positive outlook on life.

Another significant benefit of Reiki healing is its ability to improve sleep. Reiki promotes deep relaxation, which can help to improve the quality of our sleep. By reducing stress and anxiety, Reiki can also help to reduce the symptoms of insomnia and promote a more restful, rejuvenating
sleep.

Reiki healing also has immune-boosting properties. The practice of Reiki helps to promote balance and harmony within the body, which can help to boost the immune system. By reducing stress and anxiety, Reiki also helps to reduce the levels of cortisol in the body, which can have a negative impact on the immune system.

Reiki healing has also been shown to be effective in reducing pain and inflammation. The practice of Reiki promotes deep relaxation, which can help to reduce feelings of pain and discomfort. By promoting balance and harmony within the body, Reiki can also help to reduce inflammation and promote healing.

Overall, the benefits of Reiki healing are numerous and can have a profound impact on our physical, emotional, and mental well-being. By promoting relaxation, reducing stress and anxiety, improving sleep, boosting the immune system, and reducing pain and inflammation, Reiki can help us feel more balanced, centered, and at peace.

1. Everything in the universe is made up of energy, including our bodies. This energy flows through different pathways in our body and helps to maintain our physical, emotional, and spiritual well-being. When this energy is blocked or disrupted, it can lead to imbalances in our body, mind, and spirit. This can manifest as physical symptoms such as pain, fatigue, or illness, as well as emotional or spiritual issues such as anxiety, depression, or a sense of disconnect. Energy-based practices such as acupuncture, Reiki, or Tai Chi can help to unblock and balance the flow of energy in our body, promoting overall health and well-being.

2. Chakras are energy centers located along

the spine that are believed to be responsible for the flow of energy throughout the body. There are seven main chakras, each with its unique characteristics and associated colors and symbols.

The first chakra is the Root Chakra, located at the base of the spine, which is associated with grounding and survival.

The second chakra is the Sacral Chakra, located in the lower abdomen, which is associated with creativity and sexuality.

The third chakra is the Solar Plexus Chakra, located in the upper abdomen, which is associated with personal power and confidence.

The fourth chakra is the Heart Chakra, located in the center of the chest, which is associated with love and compassion.

The fifth chakra is the Throat Chakra, located in the throat, which is associated with communication and self-expression.

The sixth chakra is the Third Eye Chakra, located in the forehead, which is associated with intuition and spiritual insight.

The seventh chakra is the Crown Chakra, located at the top of the head, which is associated with enlightenment and spiritual connection.

Each chakra is linked to different organs and systems in the body and can be influenced by various factors such as emotions, thoughts, and physical health. Balancing and aligning the chakras can help to promote overall health and well-being.

3. The seven chakras are the Root Chakra, Sacral Chakra, Solar Plexus Chakra, Heart Chakra, Throat Chakra, Third Eye Chakra, and Crown Chakra. Each chakra is associated with a specific color, symbol, and set of functions. When any of these chakras become blocked or imbalanced, it can lead to physical, emotional, and spiritual issues. For example, an imbalance in the Root Chakra (located at the base of the spine) can lead to issues related to survival, such as a lack of grounding or financial instability. An imbalance in the Sacral Chakra (located in the lower abdomen) can lead to issues related to creativity and sexuality, such as a lack of passion or

pleasure in life. An imbalance in the Solar Plexus Chakra (located in the upper abdomen) can lead to issues related to personal power and confidence, such as a lack of self-esteem or a fear of taking action. An imbalance in the Heart Chakra (located in the center of the chest) can lead to issues related to love and compassion, such as a lack of empathy or difficulty forming meaningful relationships. An imbalance in the Throat Chakra (located in the throat) can lead to issues related to communication and self-expression, such as an inability to express oneself or difficulty speaking up. An imbalance in the Third Eye Chakra (located in the forehead) can lead to issues related to intuition and spiritual insight, such as a lack of clarity or a feeling of being disconnected from one's inner wisdom. An imbalance in the Crown Chakra (located at the top of the head) can lead to issues related to enlightenment and spiritual connection, such as a lack of purpose or a feeling of being disconnected from the divine. By understanding the functions of each chakra and working to balance and align them, individuals can promote overall health and well-being in all aspects of their lives.

4. Balancing and clearing the chakras is important for promoting overall health and well-being. When the chakras are balanced, energy flows freely through the body, promoting physical, emotional, and spiritual health. There are several methods for balancing the chakras, including meditation, visualization, and the use of crystals.

Meditation is a powerful tool for balancing the chakras. By focusing on the breath and directing your attention to each chakra in turn, you can help to clear blockages and promote energy flow. Visualization techniques can also be helpful, such as imagining each chakra as a spinning wheel of energy, or visualizing the corresponding color associated with each chakra.

The use of crystals is another popular method for balancing the chakras. Each chakra is associated with specific crystals that can help to clear blockages and promote balance. For example, amethyst is often used to balance the Third Eye Chakra, while rose quartz is used to balance the Heart Chakra. Placing a crystal on the corresponding chakra during meditation or carrying it with you throughout the day can help to promote balance and healing. Overall, balancing and clearing the chakras can help to promote physical health, emotional well-being, and spiritual growth. By incorporating these practices into your daily routine, you can help to maintain a healthy balance of energy throughout your body, mind, and spirit.

5. Practical exercises and techniques for working with your chakras can help you identify imbalances and blockages and promote chakra healing. Here are some examples:

1. Chakra assessment: You can start by assessing each of your chakras to determine if they are balanced or imbalanced. Stand or sit comfortably and take a few deep breaths. Focus your attention on each chakra in turn, starting with the Root Chakra and working your way up to the Crown Chakra. Notice any physical sensations, emotions, or thoughts that arise as you focus on each chakra. If you notice any areas of tension, discomfort, or imbalance, this may indicate a blockage or imbalance in that chakra.

2. Chakra clearing: Once you have identified any imbalances or blockages in your chakras, you can work on clearing them. There are many techniques for clearing the chakras, including meditation, visualization, and energy healing. One simple technique involves visualizing a bright, white light flowing through each chakra, clearing away any blockages or negative energy.

3. Reiki: Reiki is a form of energy healing that can be used to promote chakra healing. A Reiki practitioner can channel healing energy into your chakras, helping to clear blockages and promote balance. You can also learn to practice Reiki on yourself by taking a Reiki course or using self-Reiki techniques.

4. Chakra balancing: Balancing your chakras involves bringing them into harmony with each other, promoting overall health and well-being. One technique for balancing the chakras involves using sound therapy, such as listening to music that corresponds to each chakra. Another technique involves using essential oils or other aromatherapy products that correspond to each chakra. By practicing

these exercises and techniques regularly, you can promote chakra healing and maintain a healthy balance of energy throughout your body, mind, and spirit.

By understanding these concepts, you can begin to explore how to balance and clear your chakras to promote your overall health and well-being. You can also use these techniques to help others, either by becoming a Reiki practitioner or by sharing your knowledge with friends and family.

Chapter 2: Preparing for Self Reiki Healing

Before you start practicing self Reiki healing, you need to prepare yourself and your environment. This chapter will guide you through the process of creating a peaceful and relaxing space for your practice. We will also discuss the importance of setting an intention and how to do it effectively.

1. Everything in the universe is made up of energy, including our bodies. Energy can become blocked or disrupted, leading to physical, emotional, and spiritual imbalances.

2. Chakras are energy centers located along the spine that correspond to different organs and systems in the body. There are seven main chakras, each with its unique characteristics and associated colors and symbols.

3. The seven chakras are the Root Chakra, Sacral Chakra, Solar Plexus Chakra, Heart Chakra, Throat Chakra, Third Eye Chakra, and Crown Chakra. Each chakra can become blocked or imbalanced, leading to physical, emotional, and spiritual issues.

4. Balancing and clearing the chakras is important for promoting overall health and well-being. Methods for balancing your chakras include meditation, visualization, and the use of crystals.

5. Practical exercises and techniques for working with your chakras include how to identify imbalances and blockages, and how to use Reiki to promote chakra healing.

By understanding these concepts, you can begin to explore how to balance and clear your chakras to promote your overall health and well-being. You can also use these techniques to help others, either by becoming a Reiki practitioner or by sharing your knowledge with friends and family.

Creating a peaceful and relaxing space for self Reiki practice can help you to feel more comfortable and at ease while you practice. Here are some steps you can take to create a peaceful and relaxing space for your self Reiki practice:

1. Find a quiet space: Choose a quiet, private space in your home where you can practice

without being disturbed. This could be a spare room, a corner of your bedroom or living room, or even outside in nature.

2. Remove distractions: Remove any distractions that may interrupt your practice, such as your phone, computer, or television. Make sure the space is clean and free of clutter.

3. Add soothing elements: Add elements to the space that promote relaxation and calm, such as soft lighting, candles, plants, or calming music. You may also want to use essential oils or incense to create a soothing atmosphere.

4. Choose comfortable seating: Choose a comfortable chair, cushion, or mat to sit on during your self Reiki practice. Make sure you are seated in a way that supports good posture and allows you to relax.

5. Set an intention: Before you begin your self Reiki practice, take a few moments to set an intention for your practice. This could be a word or phrase that represents what you would like to cultivate during your practice,

such as peace, calm, or healing.

6. Use props: You may want to use props to support your practice, such as blankets, pillows, or bolsters. These props can help you to get comfortable and relax more deeply. Remember, the most important thing is to create a space that feels comfortable and supportive to you. Experiment with different elements until you find the right combination that helps you to feel calm, relaxed, and centered during your self Reiki practice.

Setting an intention for self Reiki practice is an important part of the practice because it helps you to focus your energy and attention on a specific goal or outcome. Here are some reasons why setting an intention is important for self Reiki practice:

1. Focus: Setting an intention helps you to focus your energy and attention on a specific goal or outcome. This can help you to stay centered and focused during your practice.

2. Clarity: An intention can help you gain clarity about what you want to achieve from your self Reiki practice. This can help you to

identify areas of your life where you need healing or support.

3. Alignment: When you set an intention, you align your energy and focus with your desired outcome. This can help to amplify your healing energy and increase the effectiveness of your practice.

4. Motivation: An intention can help to motivate you to continue your self Reiki practice, even when you feel discouraged or distracted. It can remind you of your purpose and inspire you to stay committed to your practice.

5. Manifestation: Setting an intention can help to manifest your desired outcome. By focusing your energy and attention on a specific goal, you increase the likelihood that it will manifest in your life.

Overall, setting an intention for your self Reiki practice is an important way to focus your energy and attention on a specific goal or outcome, and to increase the effectiveness of your practice. It can also help to inspire and motivate you to continue your practice over time.

Chapter 3: Learning the Reiki Hand Positions

In this chapter, we will guide you through the hand positions used in Reiki healing. These positions are designed to balance the energy flow in your body and promote healing. We will also discuss how long you should hold each position and how to adapt the hand positions to your own needs.

The length of time to hold each hand position during self Reiki healing is a matter of personal preference. Generally, it is recommended to hold each position for 3-5 minutes, or until you feel a sense of relaxation or energy shift in the area. However, some people prefer to hold each position for a shorter or longer period of time depending on their needs and preferences.

It is important to listen to your body and intuition as you practice self Reiki. If you feel called to hold a particular position for a longer period of time, trust that intuition and honor the needs of your body. Similarly, if you feel ready to move on to the next position before the recommended time, honor that as well. Remember that there is no right or wrong way to practice self Reiki, and the most important thing is to be present and attentive to your own needs and inner guidance.

Reiki hand positions are a series of specific hand placements used during a Reiki session to channel healing energy into the body. During a Reiki session, the practitioner will typically place their hands on or near various parts of the client's body, allowing the energy to flow through the hands and into the body.

The hand positions used in Reiki are based on the traditional Usui Reiki system, which uses a set of standardized hand placements. These placements are designed to cover all of the major energy centers, or chakras, in the body, as well as other areas that may need healing.

Here are some of the common hand positions used in Reiki:

1. Crown Chakra: The Crown Chakra, also known as Sahasrara, is the seventh chakra in the human body's energy system. It is located at the top of the head and is associated with spiritual awakening, enlightenment, and unity with the divine.

During a Crown Chakra meditation or energy healing session, place your hands on the top of your head to help facilitate the flow of energy through this chakra. This can help you to connect with your higher self, experience a sense of peace and oneness with the universe, and improve their overall spiritual well-being.

2. The Third Eye Chakra, also known as Ajna, is the sixth chakra in the human body's energy system. It is located in the forehead, between the eyebrows, and is associated with intuition, perception, and spiritual insight.

During a Third Eye Chakra meditation or energy healing session, place your hands on your forehead, just above the eyebrows. This can help to stimulate the energy flow through the chakra and promote a deeper sense of intuition, clarity, and inner vision. It can also help to balance and align the chakra, promoting a sense of inner harmony and peace.

Working with the Third Eye Chakra can be especially helpful for individuals who are seeking to enhance their psychic abilities or develop a stronger sense of intuition. It can also be beneficial for those who are looking to deepen their spiritual practice or gain a greater sense of connection with the divine.

3. The Throat Chakra, also known as Vishuddha, is the fifth chakra in the human body's energy system. It is located in the throat area and is associated with communication, self-expression, and creativity.

During a Throat Chakra meditation or energy healing session, place your hands on your throat. This can help to stimulate the energy flow through the chakra and promote clear communication, self-expression, and creativity. It can also help to release any blockages or tension that may be preventing the chakra from functioning properly.

Working with the Throat Chakra can be especially helpful for individuals who struggle with self-expression or have difficulty speaking their truth. It can also be beneficial for those who are involved in creative endeavors or who wish to improve their communication skills in personal or professional relationships. By balancing and aligning the Throat Chakra, individuals can experience a greater sense of authenticity, confidence, and connection with others.

4. The Heart Chakra, also known as Anahata, is the fourth chakra in the human body's energy system. It is located in the center of the chest and is associated with love, compassion, and emotional balance.

During a Heart Chakra meditation or energy healing session, place your hands on your chest, over the heart. This can help to stimulate the energy flow through the chakra and promote feelings of love, acceptance, and inner peace. It can also help to release any blockages or emotional pain that may be preventing the chakra from functioning properly.

Working with the Heart Chakra can be especially helpful for individuals who are seeking to cultivate a greater sense of self-love, compassion, and forgiveness. It can also be beneficial for those who are looking to improve their relationships with others or who are struggling with grief or heartbreak. By balancing and aligning the Heart Chakra, individuals can experience a deeper sense of connection with themselves and others, as well as a greater capacity for love and emotional wellbeing.

5. The Solar Plexus Chakra, also known as Manipura, is the third chakra in the human body's energy system. It is located in the upper abdomen, just below the ribcage, and is associated with personal power, self-esteem, and confidence.

During a Solar Plexus Chakra meditation or energy healing session, place your hands on your upper abdomen. This can help to stimulate the energy flow through the chakra and promote feelings of strength, courage, and self-assurance. It can also help to release any blockages or negative emotions that may be preventing the chakra from functioning properly.

Working with the Solar Plexus Chakra can be especially helpful for individuals who struggle with self-confidence or who have difficulty asserting themselves in personal or professional relationships. It can also be beneficial for those who are looking to improve their leadership skills or who are seeking to cultivate a greater sense of personal power and inner strength. By balancing and aligning the Solar Plexus Chakra, individuals can experience a deeper sense of self-awareness, confidence, and empowerment.

6. The Sacral Chakra, also known as Svadhisthana, is the second chakra in the human body's energy system. It is located in the lower abdomen, just below the navel, and is associated with creativity, sexuality, and emotional balance. During a Sacral Chakra meditation or energy healing session, place your hands on your lower abdomen. This can help to stimulate the energy flow through the chakra and promote feelings of pleasure, sensuality, and emotional wellbeing. It can also help to release any blockages or negative emotions that may be preventing the chakra from functioning properly.
Working with the Sacral Chakra can be especially helpful for individuals who are seeking to enhance their creativity or who are struggling with issues related to sexuality or emotional intimacy. It can also be beneficial for those who are looking to improve their

relationships with others or who are seeking to cultivate a greater sense of pleasure and enjoyment in life. By balancing and aligning the Sacral Chakra, individuals can experience a deeper sense of emotional fulfillment, creative expression, and sensual pleasure.

7. The Root Chakra, also known as Muladhara, is the first chakra in the human body's energy system. It is located at the base of the spine and is associated with a sense of grounding, stability, and security.

During a Root Chakra meditation or energy healing session, place your hands on the base of your spine. This can help to stimulate the energy flow through the chakra and promote feelings of safety, security, and stability. It can also help to release any blockages or negative emotions that may be preventing the chakra from functioning properly.

Working with the Root Chakra can be especially helpful for individuals who are struggling with issues related to safety, security, and stability, such as financial or housing insecurity, or feelings of fear or anxiety. It can also be beneficial for those who are seeking to cultivate a greater sense of grounding and connection to the physical world. By balancing and aligning the Root Chakra, individuals can experience a deeper sense of inner peace, stability, and security, as well as a greater capacity to face life's challenges with confidence and resilience.

In addition to these main hand positions, you may also use other hand positions to target specific areas of the body, such as the shoulders, knees, or feet.

It's worth noting that you may use different hand positions or variations based on how you feel. However, the basic principles of Reiki hand placement remain the same: to channel healing energy into the body and promote balance, relaxation, and well-being.

Here are the step-by-step instructions on how to perform Reiki on yourself:

1. Find a quiet, comfortable space where you won't be disturbed. Sit or lie down in a comfortable position.
2. Place your hands in the traditional Reiki hand positions, starting with your hands on

your crown chakra. You can also place your hands wherever you feel called to, depending on any specific areas that need healing.

3. Close your eyes and take a few deep breaths, allowing yourself to relax and become present in the moment.

4. Visualize a bright, healing light flowing into your body through the top of your head and filling your entire being.

5. Focus on each area of your body in turn, holding your hands in place for several minutes at each position. You can also visualize the healing light flowing through your hands and into the area of your body you are focusing on.

6. Continue holding each hand position for several minutes, until you feel a sense of relaxation and balance in the area.

7. You can also use specific Reiki symbols or mantras to enhance the healing energy and focus your intention on specific areas of healing.

8. Once you have completed all of the hand positions, take a few deep breaths and slowly come back to the present moment.

9. Take some time to rest and integrate the healing energy, and be sure to drink plenty of water to help flush out any toxins that may have been released during the session.

Remember, Reiki is a gentle, non-invasive form of healing that can be used to support your physical, emotional, and spiritual well-being. By practicing self-Reiki regularly, you can help to promote balance, relaxation, and healing in your body and mind.

Chapter 4: Starting Your Self Reiki Practice

Now that you've learned the hand positions, it's time to start your self Reiki practice. In this chapter, we will guide you through a step-by-step process of practicing self Reiki healing. We will also provide tips on how to stay focused and present during your practice.

Starting a self-Reiki practice can be a powerful way to support your physical, emotional, and spiritual well-being. Here are some ideas for getting started:

1. Set your intention: Before beginning your practice, take a few moments to set your intention for the session. This can be as simple as focusing on a specific area of your life that you want to support, such as healing from a physical ailment or finding inner peace.

2. Create a peaceful environment: Find a quiet, comfortable space where you won't be disturbed. Consider lighting candles or using essential oils to create a calming atmosphere.

3. Practice regularly: Aim to practice self-Reiki on a regular basis, such as once a day or a

few times a week. This will help you to establish a routine and experience the full benefits of Reiki.

4. Use hand positions: There are a variety of traditional hand positions used in Reiki, which involve placing your hands on different areas of your body. Experiment with different hand positions to see what feels most comfortable and effective for you.

5. Visualize healing light: As you practice self-Reiki, visualize a bright, healing light flowing into your body through the top of your head and filling your entire being. You can also visualize the healing light flowing through your hands and into the area of your body you are focusing on.

6. Incorporate Reiki symbols or mantras: Reiki symbols and mantras can be used to enhance the healing energy and focus your intention on specific areas of healing. Experiment with different symbols and mantras to see what resonates with you.

7. Be patient and open: Remember that everyone experiences Reiki differently, and it

may take time to fully experience the benefits of the practice. Stay patient and open to the process, and trust that the healing energy of Reiki is working to support your wellbeing. There are different symbols and mantras used in Reiki to enhance the healing energy and focus your intention on specific areas of healing. Here are some examples:

There are six traditional Reiki symbols, each with its unique meaning and purpose. Here are the meanings of the six Reiki symbols:

1. Cho Ku Rei: Cho Ku Rei is the power symbol and is used to amplify the Reiki energy. The symbol represents the power of the universe and the energy that flows through all things. This is one of the most commonly used Reiki symbols, and is used to increase the power or intensity of the Reiki energy. It is often used at the beginning of a Reiki session or when working on a specific area of the body. The symbol looks like a coil or spiral and is pronounced as "chou koo ray".

2. Sei Hei Ki: Sei Hei Ki is the emotional and mental symbol and is used to balance the emotions and thoughts. The symbol

represents harmony and balance. This symbol is used to promote mental and emotional healing and balance, and is often used in situations where there is emotional trauma or stress. It looks like a series of interconnected lines and is pronounced as "say hay key".

3. Hon Sha Ze Sho Nen: Hon Sha Ze Sho Nen is the distance symbol and is used to send Reiki energy across time and space. The symbol represents the interconnectedness of all things. This symbol is used to send Reiki energy across time and space, making it a useful tool for distant healing. It looks like a series of interconnected triangles and is pronounced as "hawn shaw zay show nen".

4. Dai Ko Myo: Dai Ko Myo is the master symbol and is used for spiritual healing and enlightenment. The symbol represents the ultimate truth and the realization of the true self. This symbol is used to promote spiritual healing and connection, and is often used in situations where the practitioner is working on deep-seated or long-standing issues. It looks like a series of interconnected circles and is pronounced as "dye ko mee oh".

5. Raku: Raku is the grounding symbol and is used to ground the energy after a Reiki session. The symbol represents the connection between the physical and spiritual worlds.

6. Zonar: Zonar is a non-traditional Reiki symbol that is used to clear and balance the chakras. The symbol represents the flow of energy through the body.

CHO KU REI   SEI HE KI   HON SHA ZE SHO NEN

DAI KO MYO   DAI KO MYO   RAKU

Each of these symbols has its unique energy and purpose, and they are used by Reiki practitioners to enhance the Reiki healing process.

In addition to symbols, there are also mantras that can be used in Reiki practice. Some examples include:

1. Om, also written as Aum, is a sacred sound and a powerful universal mantra in Hinduism, Buddhism, and other spiritual traditions. It represents the sound of the universe and is often chanted during meditation, yoga, and other spiritual practices.

The sound "Om" is believed to be the primordial sound of the universe, the sound that was present at the time of creation. It is said to vibrate at the same frequency as the universe itself, and chanting it can help to align one's own vibration with that of the universe.

Om is often chanted at the beginning and end of yoga classes and meditation sessions, as well as during breathing exercises. The sound is believed to promote relaxation, inner peace, and spiritual awakening. It can also help to calm the mind, reduce stress and anxiety, and enhance one's focus and concentration.

Chanting Om is a simple yet powerful practice that can be done anywhere and at any time. It can be chanted out loud or silently, and is often repeated several times in succession. By chanting Om and focusing on the sound and vibration, individuals can connect with their inner selves and experience a greater sense of peace, harmony, and spiritual awareness.

2. So Hum is a mantra that is commonly used in meditation practices to promote self-awareness and inner reflection. It is a Sanskrit phrase that means "I am that" or "I am that which I seek". It is pronounced as "so hum" and is often chanted silently or out loud during meditation.

The mantra is based on the belief that we are all connected to the universe and that we are all part of a larger whole. By chanting So Hum, individuals can tap into this sense of interconnectedness and reflect on their true nature and purpose.

The sound "so" is associated with inhalation, while "hum" is associated with exhalation. As individuals chant the mantra, they may focus on their breath and the sound of the mantra, allowing them to enter a state of deep relaxation and inner peace.

So Hum is often used as a tool for self-discovery and personal growth. By reflecting on the meaning of the mantra and chanting it during meditation, individuals can gain a deeper understanding of themselves and their connection to the universe. It can also help to reduce stress and anxiety, promote a sense of calm and relaxation, and enhance one's focus and concentration.

Overall, So Hum is a powerful mantra that can help individuals to connect with their inner selves and tap into their true nature and purpose.

3. Om Mani Padme Hum is a popular mantra in Tibetan Buddhism that is believed to promote compassion and healing. It is a powerful mantra that is chanted during meditation, prayer, and other spiritual practices.

The mantra consists of six syllables, which are pronounced as "om mani padme hum". Each syllable is said to have its own unique meaning and significance.

"Om" represents the sound of the universe, while "mani" means jewel and is associated with the quality of compassion. "Padme" means lotus and is associated with purity and enlightenment, while "hum" is said to represent the mind and its transformation. Together, the mantra is believed to invoke the energy of compassion and healing, allowing individuals to connect with their inner selves and experience a greater sense of peace, harmony, and spiritual awareness.

Om Mani Padme Hum is often chanted during meditation, with individuals focusing on the sound and vibration of the mantra as they breathe deeply and relax. It can also be used as a tool for healing, with individuals visualizing the energy of the mantra flowing through their body and promoting healing and rejuvenation.

The mantra is associated with the bodhisattva Avalokiteshvara, who is revered as a symbol of compassion and mercy in Tibetan Buddhism. By chanting Om Mani Padme Hum, individuals can connect with the energy of this compassionate deity and invoke his blessings and protection.

Overall, Om Mani Padme Hum is a powerful mantra that is widely used in Tibetan Buddhism and other spiritual traditions. It is believed to promote compassion, healing, and spiritual awakening, and can be a powerful tool for personal growth and transformation.

Chapter 5: Troubleshooting Your Self Reiki Practice

In this chapter, we will address common issues that arise during self Reiki healing. We will provide solutions to help you overcome these challenges and get the most out of your practice.

If you're experiencing challenges with your self-Reiki practice, here are some common issues and solutions:

1. Difficulty feeling the Reiki energy: Some people may find it challenging to feel the Reiki energy during their practice, especially when they are first starting out. One solution is to focus on your breath and visualization techniques to help you connect with the energy. You can also try different hand positions and experiment with different symbols and mantras to see what feels most effective for you.

2. Feeling overwhelmed or anxious during the practice: If you find yourself feeling overwhelmed or anxious during your self-Reiki practice, try to focus on your breath and

visualization techniques to help you relax. You can also try using calming essential oils or playing soothing music to help create a more peaceful atmosphere.

3. Experiencing physical discomfort: If you experience physical discomfort during your Reiki practice, such as stiffness or pain in your hands or arms, try adjusting your hand positions or taking breaks as needed. You can also try using props, such as pillows or bolsters, to help support your body during the practice.

4. Struggling to maintain a consistent practice: If you find it challenging to maintain a consistent self-Reiki practice, try setting a regular schedule and setting reminders for yourself. You can also try incorporating Reiki into other parts of your daily routine, such as during your morning or evening ritual.

5. Feeling unsure about your technique: If you're feeling unsure about your technique or would like additional guidance, consider working with a Reiki practitioner or taking a Reiki course. This can help you deepen your understanding of the practice and provide you

with additional tools and resources to support your self-Reiki practice.

Chapter 6: Incorporating Reiki into Your Daily Life

We will discuss how to incorporate Reiki into your daily life. We will provide tips on how to use Reiki for stress relief, pain management, and overall well-being. We will also discuss how to use Reiki to enhance your meditation practice and deepen your spiritual connection.

Reiki is a versatile practice that can be incorporated into your daily life in a variety of ways. Here are some ideas to get started:

1. Morning routine: Incorporate Reiki into your morning routine by spending a few minutes practicing self-Reiki before you start your day. This can help you feel more grounded and centered as you move into your day.

2. Mindful eating: Use Reiki to infuse your food and drinks with healing energy. You can do this by holding your hands over your food or drink for a few moments before consuming it, or by visualizing Reiki energy flowing into the food or drink as you prepare it.

3. Bedtime ritual: Incorporate Reiki into your bedtime ritual by practicing self-Reiki before you go to sleep. This can help you relax and unwind after a long day, and promote a restful night's sleep.

4. Work breaks: Take short Reiki breaks throughout the day to recharge and refresh. This can involve practicing self-Reiki for a few minutes, or simply taking a few deep breaths and visualizing Reiki energy flowing through your body.

5. Healing intentions: Use Reiki to set healing intentions for yourself or others. You can do this by focusing your Reiki energy on a specific area of your body or by sending Reiki energy to someone who is in need of healing.

Remember that Reiki is a flexible practice that can be adapted to suit your individual needs and preferences. Experiment with different ways of incorporating Reiki into your daily life and see what works best for you.

Chapter 7 Reiki For Pets

Example Reiki for a dog:

Samantha, a Reiki practitioner, had always been interested in working with animals and felt a strong connection to them. One day, she received a call from a friend who was concerned about her dog, Max. Max had been experiencing chronic pain and discomfort, and traditional veterinary treatments had not been effective in relieving his symptoms.

Samantha offered to provide Reiki to Max to see if it could help him find some relief. She arrived at her friend's home and sat down on the floor next to Max, who was lying on his bed. Samantha explained to her friend that Reiki is a form of energy healing that works to balance the body's energy system and promote relaxation and healing.

Samantha began the session by placing her hands on Max's body, starting at his head and moving down to his feet. She focused on sending healing energy to any areas where she sensed blockages or tension. Max seemed to sense the energy and relaxed into the treatment, letting out a contented sigh.

As the session continued, Samantha noticed that Max's breathing became deeper and more relaxed, and his body seemed to release some of the tension it had been holding. She continued to work on Max's energy, allowing him to receive the healing he needed.

After the session was complete, Samantha explained to her friend that Max may feel some shifts in his energy and that it was important to give him time to rest and integrate the healing.

The next day, Samantha received a call from her friend, who was amazed at the improvement in Max's condition. He was more active, had a better appetite, and seemed to be experiencing less pain.

Samantha was thrilled to hear the news and felt grateful to have been able to provide Max with the healing he needed. She knew that Reiki had the power to help animals like Max find relief and healing, and she was committed to continuing her work in this area.

Example of Reiki for a cat:

Laura was a Reiki practitioner who had always been drawn to working with animals. One day, a friend reached out to her about her cat, Fluffy, who was experiencing anxiety and stress due to a recent move. Fluffy had been hiding under the bed and refusing to come out, and her friend was worried about her well-being.

Laura offered to provide Reiki to Fluffy in hopes that it could help her find some peace and relaxation. She arrived at her friend's home and sat down on the floor next to Fluffy, who was hiding under the bed. Laura explained to her friend that Reiki is a form of energy healing that works on balancing the body's energy system and promoting relaxation and healing.

Laura started the session by placing her hands on Fluffy's body, starting at her head and moving down to her tail. She focused on sending healing energy to any areas where she sensed blockages or tension. Fluffy seemed to sense the energy and relaxed, peeking out from under the bed to look at

Laura.

As the session continued, Laura noticed that Fluffy's breathing became deeper and more relaxed, and her body seemed to release some of the tension it had been holding. Laura continued to work on Fluffy's energy, allowing her to receive the healing she needed.

After the session was complete, Laura explained to her friend that Fluffy may feel some shifts in her energy and that it was important to give her time to rest and integrate the healing. The next day, Laura received a call from her friend, who was amazed at the improvement in Fluffy's behavior. She was more active, playing with her toys, and seemed to be much more relaxed.

Laura was thrilled to hear the news and felt grateful to have been able to provide Fluffy with the healing she needed. She knew that Reiki had the power to help animals like Fluffy find relief and healing, and she was committed to continuing her work with animals in the future.

In this final chapter, we will discuss performing Reiki on a pet which is similar to performing Reiki on a human.

Here are some steps to follow:

1. Creating a calm environment is an important step in helping your pet relax and reduce stress. Pets can be sensitive to their environment and may feel anxious or overwhelmed in noisy, chaotic spaces. By creating a calm and quiet environment, you can help your pet feel more at ease and promote relaxation and wellbeing.

To create a calm environment for your pet, start by finding a quiet and peaceful space.

This could be a cozy corner in your home, a comfortable bed, or a favorite spot in your backyard. Pay attention to your pet's preferences and choose a location where they feel safe and comfortable.

Make sure the space is free from distractions and noise. Turn off the TV or radio, close the windows to block out outside noise, and minimize any other sources of disturbance. If your pet is easily distracted by movement or activity, consider using a divider or screen to create a separate space.

You can also use calming scents, such as lavender or chamomile, to help create a more relaxing environment. These scents can be used in diffusers or sprays, or you can use natural remedies like dried herbs or essential oils.

In addition to creating a calm environment, you can also help your pet relax by incorporating calming activities into their routine. This could include gentle massage, soothing music, or guided relaxation exercises.

By creating a calm and peaceful environment for your pet, you can help them feel more relaxed and at ease. This can lead to improved wellbeing, reduced stress, and a happier, healthier pet.

2. Connecting with your pet is an important aspect of Reiki therapy. It helps to establish a bond of trust and mutual understanding between you and your pet, which is essential

for the Reiki session to be effective.

Before beginning the Reiki session, take a few moments to connect with your pet. This can involve petting and talking to your pet, or simply sitting quietly beside them. Try to be present in the moment and focus your attention on your pet. This will help to create a calm and relaxed atmosphere, which is conducive to the Reiki energy flow.

As you connect with your pet, pay attention to their body language and behavior. This can give you important clues about their emotional and physical state, and can help you to tailor the Reiki session to their specific needs.

When you are ready to begin the Reiki session, take a deep breath and focus your attention on your pet's energy field. Visualize the Reiki energy flowing from your hands into your pet's body, filling them with healing energy and promoting balance and harmony.

Throughout the Reiki session, continue to connect with your pet and be present in the moment. This will help to ensure that the Reiki energy is flowing smoothly and effectively, and that your pet is receiving maximum benefit from the treatment.

After the Reiki session is complete, take a few moments to connect with your pet again. This can help to ground and center them, and can also help to deepen the bond of trust and understanding between you and your pet.

By connecting with your pet before and after the Reiki session, you can create a positive and healing experience for both you and your pet. This can lead to improved wellbeing, reduced stress, and a stronger bond between you and your furry friend.

3. Beginning the Reiki session is a crucial part of the process that requires patience, focus, and sensitivity to your pet's needs and preferences. The way you begin the session can set the tone for the entire experience, so it's important to take your time and make sure you and your pet are both comfortable and relaxed.

To start the session, find a comfortable position for both you and your pet. You can sit or lie down, whatever feels most comfortable for both of you. Place your hands on or near your pet's body, depending on their comfort level. If your pet is not comfortable with physical touch, you can use distance healing techniques, such as visualizing the Reiki energy flowing from your hands to your pet's body.

Once you have established the physical connection, close your eyes and take a few deep breaths. Clear your mind and focus on your intention to heal and help your pet. Visualize the Reiki energy flowing from your hands into your pet's body, filling them with healing energy and promoting balance and harmony.

As you continue the Reiki session, pay attention to your pet's reactions and behavior. They may become more relaxed, start to purr, or fall asleep. Alternatively, they may become restless or fidgety, which could indicate a blockage or tension in their energy field. If this happens, adjust your hand position or use different Reiki techniques to help release the blockage and restore balance.

Throughout the session, continue to focus

your intention and visualize the Reiki energy flowing smoothly and effectively. Trust your intuition and let the energy guide you. Remember to stay present in the moment and remain open to any insights or messages that may come through during the session.

When the session is complete, take a few moments to reconnect with your pet and ground them with your energy. This can help them to integrate the healing energy and promote a sense of calm and well-being.

Overall, beginning the Reiki session is a gentle and nurturing process that requires patience, sensitivity, and a deep connection with your pet. By following these guidelines, you can create a positive and healing experience for both you and your furry friend.

4. Using hand positions is a fundamental aspect of Reiki therapy, whether it's for self-healing, healing others, or healing pets. By placing your hands on or near your pet's body, you can channel the healing energy of Reiki and promote balance and harmony in their energy field.

When using hand positions on your pet, it's important to follow some basic guidelines to ensure that the session is safe, effective, and comfortable for both you and your pet.

Start by placing your hands on your pet's body, starting at the head or neck and working your way down. Use a light touch and apply gentle pressure, following the natural contours of your pet's body. You can use hand positions similar to those used in self-Reiki or Reiki on humans, such as placing your hands on the ears, forehead, chest, stomach, or limbs.

As you move your hands around your pet's body, pay attention to their reactions and behavior. They may become more relaxed, start to purr, or fall asleep. Alternatively, they may become restless or fidgety, which could indicate a blockage or tension in their energy field. If this happens, adjust your hand position or use different Reiki techniques to help release the blockage and restore balance. You can also use your intuition to guide you to the areas of your pet's body that need the most attention. Trust your instincts and let the Reiki energy flow through your hands to

where it's needed most.
Remember to take breaks as needed, especially if your pet becomes restless or uncomfortable. You can also use distance healing techniques or Reiki symbols if your pet is not comfortable with physical touch.

In general, using hand positions is a gentle and nurturing process that can help to promote a sense of calm and wellbeing in your pet. By following these guidelines, you can create a positive and healing experience for both you and your furry friend.

5. It's important to trust your intuition and let it guide you as you perform Reiki on your pet. Your intuition is a powerful tool that can help you to tune into your pet's energy field and identify areas that need attention.

When performing Reiki on your pet, pay attention to their reactions and behavior. If your pet seems uncomfortable or restless, it may be an indication that they need you to adjust your hand positions or take a break. Your intuition can help you to identify the root cause of your pet's discomfort and suggest the best course of action.

For example, if your pet seems to be avoiding a particular area of their body where you're placing your hands, it may be a sign that they're experiencing discomfort or pain in that area. You can adjust your hand position to a nearby area or try a different Reiki technique to help release the tension or blockage.

Similarly, if your pet becomes restless or fidgety during the session, it may be a sign that they're feeling overwhelmed or overstimulated by the Reiki energy. In this case, you can take a break or pause the session to allow your pet to rest and integrate the healing energy.

By following your intuition and being attuned to your pet's needs and preferences, you can create a positive and healing experience for both you and your pet. Remember to approach the Reiki session with an open mind and heart, and trust that the energy will flow where it's needed most.

6. Ending a Reiki session is just as important as starting one. When you are ready to conclude your Reiki session with your pet, it's

essential to follow a few guidelines to ensure that you and your pet feel complete and grounded.

Firstly, thank your pet for sharing the Reiki experience with you. Express your gratitude for the opportunity to connect with them on a deeper level and offer them a few words of love and appreciation.

Next, take a few moments to ground yourself before moving on with your day. Grounding involves bringing your awareness back into your physical body and connecting with the earth's energy. You can do this by taking a few deep breaths, visualizing roots growing from your feet into the earth, or standing barefoot on the ground.

It's also a good idea to check in with your pet and observe how they're feeling after the session. They may be more relaxed or sleepy than usual, or they may be more alert and active. Pay attention to their behavior and make any necessary adjustments to their routine or environment to support their healing process.

Finally, remember to take care of yourself after the session. Reiki can be a powerful and transformative experience, and it's essential to nurture yourself and integrate the energy into your being. Drink plenty of water, rest if needed, and give yourself time to reflect on the experience.

Conclusion

In conclusion, ending a Reiki session with your pet is a simple yet essential process that can help to solidify the healing experience and promote balance and harmony in your pet's energy field. By following these guidelines, you can create a positive and nurturing experience for both you and your pet.

Remember that Reiki can be a powerful tool for promoting relaxation, healing, and well-being in pets as well as humans. With practice and patience, you can develop a deep connection with your pet and use Reiki to support their overall health and happiness.

Practicing self Reiki can be a life-changing experience that can help you to connect with your inner self, promote healing, and enhance your overall well-being. By following the tips and techniques outlined in this e-book, you can start your own self Reiki practice and experience the benefits for yourself.

It's important to remember that Reiki healing is a personal journey, and that everyone's experience will be unique. Be patient and gentle with yourself as you explore this new practice, and don't be afraid to experiment with different techniques and approaches to find what works best for you.

Regular practice is key to getting the most out of your Reiki healing journey. Try to set aside time each day to practice, even if it's just for a few minutes. Over time, you'll begin to notice the positive effects of Reiki on your mind, body, and spirit.

Remember that Reiki healing is not a substitute for medical treatment, and you should always consult with a qualified healthcare professional before making any changes to your health routine.

In summary, practicing self Reiki can be a powerful tool for promoting healing, reducing stress, and enhancing overall well-being. With dedication, patience, and an open mind, you can start your own self Reiki practice and experience the transformative power of this ancient healing art.

About the Author

Kulada is a highly experienced and qualified Reiki Master with over 30 years of practice in the field of energy healing. Her passion for Reiki was sparked at a young age, and she has since dedicated her life to sharing the healing benefits of this ancient practice with others.

Kulada has completed extensive training in a variety of Reiki modalities, including Usui, Karuna, and Holy Fire Reiki. Her deep understanding of the human body and energy system allows her to provide personalized and effective treatments to her clients.

As a female Reiki Master, Kulada brings a nurturing and compassionate energy to her practice, creating a safe and supportive environment for healing to occur. She is known for her intuitive abilities and gentle touch, and has helped many clients overcome physical, emotional, and spiritual challenges.

In addition to her Reiki practice, Kulada is also a dedicated teacher and mentor, offering training and certification programs for those looking to deepen their knowledge of Reiki and become practitioners themselves.

Through her work, Kulada is committed to helping others connect with their inner wisdom, find balance and harmony in their lives, and experience the transformative power of Reiki.

Made in the USA
Columbia, SC
30 May 2023

d5e95551-c034-44fb-8ee3-67344335af86R01